Times Square

A New York State Number Book

Written by Ann E. Burg and Illustrated by Maureen K. Brookfield

My heartfelt thanks to Star and Pat from the Shaker Heritage Foundation for their warm Shaker welcome; to Deb Callery at the Johnstown Public Library for helping me discover baseball history in my own backyard, and to Darlene, Michelle, and Dana of the deBeer factory. Thanks to Betsy Travis from the Potsdam Public Library, and Carol at the Congressional Medal of Honor office. A warm thanks to Winnie DeWitt West and her family for sharing their childhood memories, and to my busy brother-in-law, Dr. Steven Burg. A special thanks to my family for accompanying me on all my fact-finding adventures!

—A.B.

Sleeping Bear Press™

315 E. Eisenhower Parkway, Suite 200
Ann Arbor, MI 48108
www.sleepingbearpress.com

Sleeping Bear Press is an imprint of Gale, a part of Cengage Learning.

Printed and bound in the United States.

10 9 8 7 6 5 4 3 2

Library of Congress Cataloging-in-Publication Data

Burg, Ann E.
Times Square : a New York state number book / written by Ann E. Burg ;
illustrated by Maureen K. Brookfield.
p. cm.
Includes bibliographical references and index.
ISBN 978-1-58536-195-3 (alk. paper)
1. Counting—Juvenile literature. 2. New York (State)—Juvenile literature.
I. Brookfield, Maureen K., 1947- ill. II. Title.

F119.3.B875 2005
974.7—dc22   2005005890

Printed by Bang Printing, Brainerd, MN. 2nd Ptg, 07/2011

From the mid nineteenth century to the mid twentieth century many children in rural areas of New York were educated in a one-room schoolhouse. In this one room, students from grades one through eight gathered to study some of the same subjects you study. During recess children played tag, hide-and-seek, and other games still popular today. Up until 1953 boys and girls who attended the Woodinville School in Dutchess County played baseball in a nearby cow pasture or picked wild berries and honeysuckle. Their favorite hot lunches were hot dogs or macaroni and cheese.

Attendance in a school has not always been mandatory and in some areas attendance changed according to the season. In the 1840s boys who were needed on the farm might only go to school in the winter when they did not have as many chores. By law, students between the ages of four and twenty-one *could* attend school; however, school attendance in New York was not mandatory until 1874.

one
1

Now we'll start at 1 - 2 - 3,
so come along and count with me.
We've so much more to celebrate
in beautiful, bountiful New York State!

1 room and 1 teacher
in 1 little house of brick,
teaching many lively children
reading, 'riting, and 'rithmetic.

Did you ever see a lion
on a busy city street?
If you visit New York City,
there are **2** that you can meet!

If you visit the New York Public Library at Fifth Avenue and 42nd Street in New York City, you'll see two majestic marble lions on either side of the entry stairs. Originally called Leo Astor and Leo Lenox after the founders of the library, the lions are now referred to as **Patience** and **Fortitude**. Fiorello La Guardia, the mayor of New York City from 1933 to 1945, believed that New Yorkers needed patience and fortitude to survive difficult times. People agreed and the names endured.

In addition to Patience and Fortitude, live lions marched in the Macy's Thanksgiving Day Parades of 1925 and 1926. The Macy's Parade continues to this day, but the wild animals were banished because they frightened children. Now, if you want to hear a lion roar in New York, you'll need to visit one of our many state zoos!

two
2

A scallop is a shellfish made of two hinged shells. These double-shelled creatures are known as bivalves. The scallop is one of the few bivalves that have eyes. Dozens of tiny blue eyes are dotted along the edges of the scallop. These eyes help the scallop to detect changes in light and movement, warning them about approaching predators. If scallops need to move, they propel themselves forward by quickly opening and closing their hinged shells.

The scallop was declared our state shell in 1988.

three
3

Shy bay scallops
hide in their bed beneath the sea.
Count them as you find them—
1 - 2 - 3!

Millions of years before jeeps, motorcycles, and sport utility vehicles traveled the New York State Thruway, sea scorpions scrabbled the bottom of the shallow, briny waters that once covered our state. The sea scorpion looked like an overgrown lobster. It had a segmented body, jointed legs, and large snapping pincers that it used to terrorize and capture its prey.

The best examples of sea scorpion fossils are found on a stretch of rock between Poughkeepsie and New York City, which has been called the "sea scorpion graveyard." Because the first recorded sea scorpion fossil was found in New York, we declared it our state fossil in 1984.

4 fragile fossils
tell secrets from long ago,
when sea scorpions scuttled the waters
from Poughkeepsie to Buffalo.

four

4

New York City is divided into five administrative districts (boroughs), each of which reflect the unique spirit of those who live there. Every year, runners from around the world gather to take part in the New York City Marathon, whose course winds its way through these five boroughs. Thousands of athletes run from **Staten Island**, to **Brooklyn**, and on into **Queens**. They then loop into **Manhattan** and through the **Bronx**, returning to Manhattan to cross the finish line in Central Park.

Running through the five boroughs of New York City, marathoners experience the amazing diversity and dynamic spirit of New York's most famous city.

five

5

These **5** boroughs of New York City
rumble with the beat
of thirty thousand runners
stomping their sneakered feet!

"On your mark—get set—
...GO!!!"

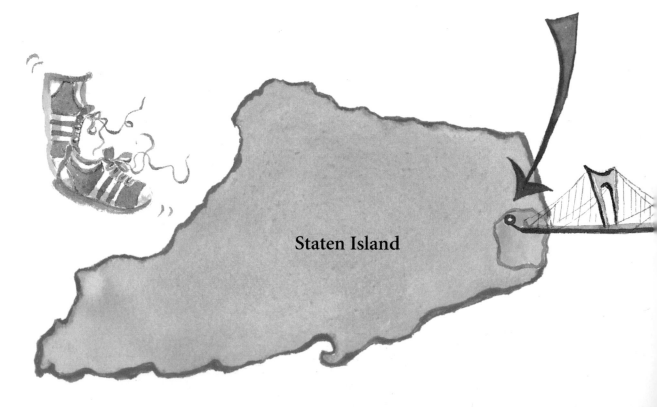

Staten Island

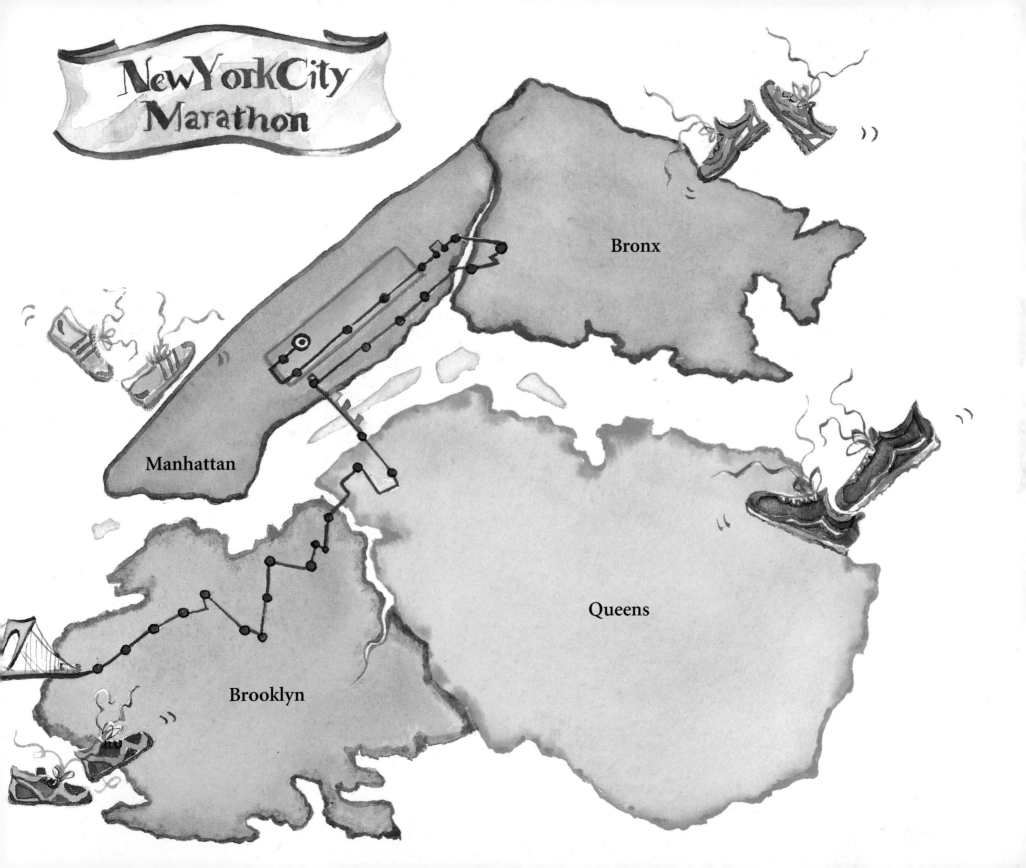

New York City Marathon

6 long, narrow lakes
are like the fingers of a hand,
opened wide to bless
this lush and fertile land.

Canandaigua Lake

Keuka Lake

Seneca Lake

One of the prettiest places in New York is the Finger Lakes region located in the central part of our state. Here, apple orchards, vineyards, and dairy farms surround narrow glacial lakes, sparkling streams, glistening waterfalls, and magnificent gorges. From east to west the six major Finger Lakes are Skaneateles, Owasco, Cayuga, Seneca, Keuka, and Canandaigua. There are several smaller lakes as well.

According to Iroquois legend the hand imprint of the Great Spirit formed these lakes. How do *you* think these long, narrow lakes were formed?

Skaneateles Lake

Owasco Lake

Cayuga Lake

six

6

Native Americans who lived in New York before the arrival of the first European settlers lived close to the earth. They were appreciative of their resources and called their primary crops of corn, beans, and squash "The Three Sisters." These crops were often planted together; bean plants would climb the growing cornstalks; and the large, low leaves of the squash provided shade for the soil, and discouraged weeds.

Because nothing was ever wasted, the husks of corn were used to make household supplies such as baskets, moccasins, bed mats, and even dolls!

seven

7

7 cornhusk dolls
are resting in the shade.
Look very, very closely
to see how they were made!

8 slices of pie
topped with ice cream luscious and cold.
Just another New York invention—
scrumptious pie à la mode!

à

According to local legend, Professor Charles Watson Townsend liked to dine at the Hotel Cambridge in Cambridge, New York. He often ordered the same dessert, a slice of pie with a dollop of ice cream. One day a Mrs. Berry Hall asked Professor Townsend what this pie-and-ice-cream dessert was called. Since the dessert had no name, she dubbed it "Pie à la Mode."

Sometime later Professor Townsend was dining at Delmonico's, a very famous restaurant in New York City. He asked for pie à la mode and feigned shock when such a famous restaurant in such a big city did not carry a dessert that was so easily ordered in a small town in upstate New York. A reporter for the *New York Sun* overheard the conversation and the next day the newspaper carried an article about pie à la mode. National newspapers picked up the story, and pie à la mode became the nation's trendiest dessert!

eight
8

L. Frank Baum, author of *The Wizard of Oz*, was born on May 15, 1856 in Chittenango. Every year thousands of fans visit Baum's hometown for the annual Oz Fest, a celebration of all things OZ. Activities include a parade and costume contests. The town is also home to the L. Frank Baum Oz Museum.

Many other well-known children's authors can claim New York hometowns, including Bruce Coville (Syracuse), Madeleine L'Engle (New York City), and Maurice Sendak (Brooklyn). Do you know the books for which they are famous? Who is your favorite New York author?

nine

9

9 bricks on this winding road:
Follow them and you'll find
a wizard, a tin man, a scarecrow,
and a very cowardly lion.

10 precision dancers
standing in a line
link arms and kick in unison
when they perform at Christmastime!

ROCKETT

Originally known as the "Missouri Rockets," the Radio City Rockettes first came to New York in 1932. At that time there were only 16 dancers. Now numbering 36, the amazing Rockettes swirl, kick, and sparkle in completely synchronized motions. Most famous for their annual Christmas performances at Radio City Music Hall, the Rockettes also march in city streets during the Macy's Thanksgiving Day Parade and add sparkle to the yearly Tree Lighting Ceremony at Rockefeller Center. In 2001 the Rockettes dazzled down the steps of the Lincoln Memorial in Washington, D.C.

ten
10

The United States Quarters program was initiated to honor the unique contributions of each state, and each quarter is individually designed. New York's quarter shows the Statue of Liberty against an outline of the state. Eleven stars, representing the number of states when New York joined the Union, are positioned along the rim, and the words "Gateway to Freedom" appear to the right of the Statue of Liberty. If you look carefully, you will see a line that traces the route of the Hudson River and the Erie Canal.

Other designs were also considered, including one of Federal Hall where George Washington took his oath of office. It was decided, however, that the chosen design best captured the essence of New York. What do you think?

11 stars on the quarter
that honors New York State,
the eleventh to join the Union
in July of 1788.

eleven
11

Count the paintbrushes
and you'll find **12**,
rinsed and drying
on a shelf.

The beauty of our state has inspired many artists. In the 1820s a group of artists who called themselves the Hudson River School of Landscape Painting used light and precise details to capture the unspoiled beauty of our young nation. Other celebrated New York artists include Grandma Moses and Norman Rockwell.

Born Anna Mary Robertson, Grandma Moses did not begin painting until she was in her seventies! Because her hands hurt too much to do needlepoint, her family persuaded her to capture her memories in paint instead of thread.

Unlike Grandma Moses, Norman Rockwell knew from a very young age that he wanted to be an artist. Four of Rockwell's most famous paintings are called the *Four Freedoms*. In a speech given to Congress in 1941, President Franklin Roosevelt outlined the four essential human freedoms: freedom of speech, freedom of religion, freedom from want, and freedom from fear. Rockwell visually captured these abstract concepts by painting scenes from everyday American life.

twelve
12

The Catskill Mountains once provided a fertile hunting ground for Native Americans who tracked the deer, bear, and turkeys who still roam these hills. Later, the region was dotted with farms and apple orchards. The well-known Jonathan apple was first produced in Woodstock, a small hamlet in the shadow of the Catskill Mountains. Although no longer grown there, the Jonathan apple continues to be produced in orchards around the world.

Generations of artists, poets, and musicians have also discovered and claimed the gentle wilderness of the Catskill Mountain region. In 1969 thousands of people gathered for the Woodstock Festival, a marathon concert that was held in Bethel, not far from Woodstock. For three days, songs of peace and of protest rocked the quiet countryside.

The Woodstock Festival has eclipsed the earlier history of Woodstock, but its pastoral heritage lives on in the Jonathan apple.

twenty
20

We've counted cornhusk dolls
and followed the yellow brick road.
We found two lions on a city street
and fossils from long ago.
Now let's count by tens,
starting with number 20.
There's so much more to learn
about New York's land of plenty!

Tucked in the Catskill Mountains
on this ancient apple tree,
count **20** native New York apples—
now grown across the sea.

These **30** oval boxes
for buttons, pins, or twine
were made by the Shakers
who valued practical design.

Founded by Mother Ann Lee, the Shakers were a religious community who left England in 1774 to escape persecution. They established their first settlement in what is now Colonie, New York, and at one time had 6,000 followers in 19 different communities.

Both industrious and devout, the Shakers believed that work was a form of worship. The simple, graceful furniture that they designed and their uncluttered use of space has become a popular decorating style. It is important to remember, however, that the Shakers did not intend to make a fashion statement. The beautiful objects that they created reflect their devout belief that even the most common button box or rocking chair was an opportunity to attain perfection. While their hands worked diligently, they were giving their hearts to God.

thirty
30

New York is baseball country! Fans of the American League root for the Yankees, while fans of the National League cheer for the Mets. When both home teams play each other in the World Series, it's called a *subway series*. Subway series are exciting for all fans, and New Yorkers everywhere get involved. Even Patience and Fortitude have been photographed sporting the caps of their favorite New York team! But New York was involved with baseball long before the arrival of the Yankees and the Mets.

In 1889 Jacob deBeer, a leather tanner, began manufacturing baseballs in a converted barn in Johnstown, New York. The deBeer baseball factory was a family business and everyone got involved. Jacob's wife, Jenny, originated the method of stitching the ball cover, and years later, Jacob's grandson, Frederick, invented the "Clincher" softball which was stitched on the inside.

There are 108 stitches in a baseball and 88 in a softball.

forty
40

40 red-stitched baseballs
hurled, grounded, or spun:
Three players on three bases root
for a **GRAND SLAM** homerun!

50 glass bottles of milk,
cold, fresh, and delicious.
Start your day with a drink
that's both tasty and nutritious!

Milk was declared our official state beverage in 1981 and dairy farms can be found throughout our state.

In the early years of milk production, people who did not live on farms relied on the milkman to deliver directly to their homes. Pulling up in his horse-drawn wagon, he would stop and ladle milk from his own milk can into the containers of his customers.

Although Alexander Campbell of Brooklyn patented a glass milk bottle in 1878, Dr. Hervey Thatcher of Potsdam is generally considered the inventor of the modern milk bottle, patented in 1884. It's been said that Dr. Thatcher was out walking when he saw a little girl drop her rag doll into a milkman's milk can. The milkman fished the doll out, and continued ladling milk from the can. Horrified at this, Dr. Thatcher hurried home to design a more sanitary method of milk delivery!

fifty

50

The secret as to why the Dutch wore wooden shoes may be found in the formal name of Holland, the *Netherlands*. "Nether" means below or under—and much of the land of the Netherlands is below sea level. The land that the Dutch were accustomed to farming was wet; wooden shoes helped keep their feet dry.

Although the Dutch only ruled New York for a short time, we can trace numerous examples of their influence on our language and culture. The gabled roof, the shutter, and the stoop are architectural details borrowed from the Dutch. Many place names also reflect our Dutch heritage. Can you translate *Breukelyn* and *Haarlem*? Look up the words "waffle" and "coleslaw," "snoop" and "spook." Language changes and adapts according to the community it serves. What words do you know that our early ancestors would not?

sixty

60

60 wooden shoes
(three pairs to a row)
remind us of the settlers
who came here long ago.

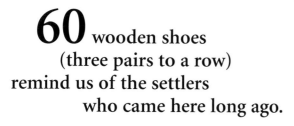

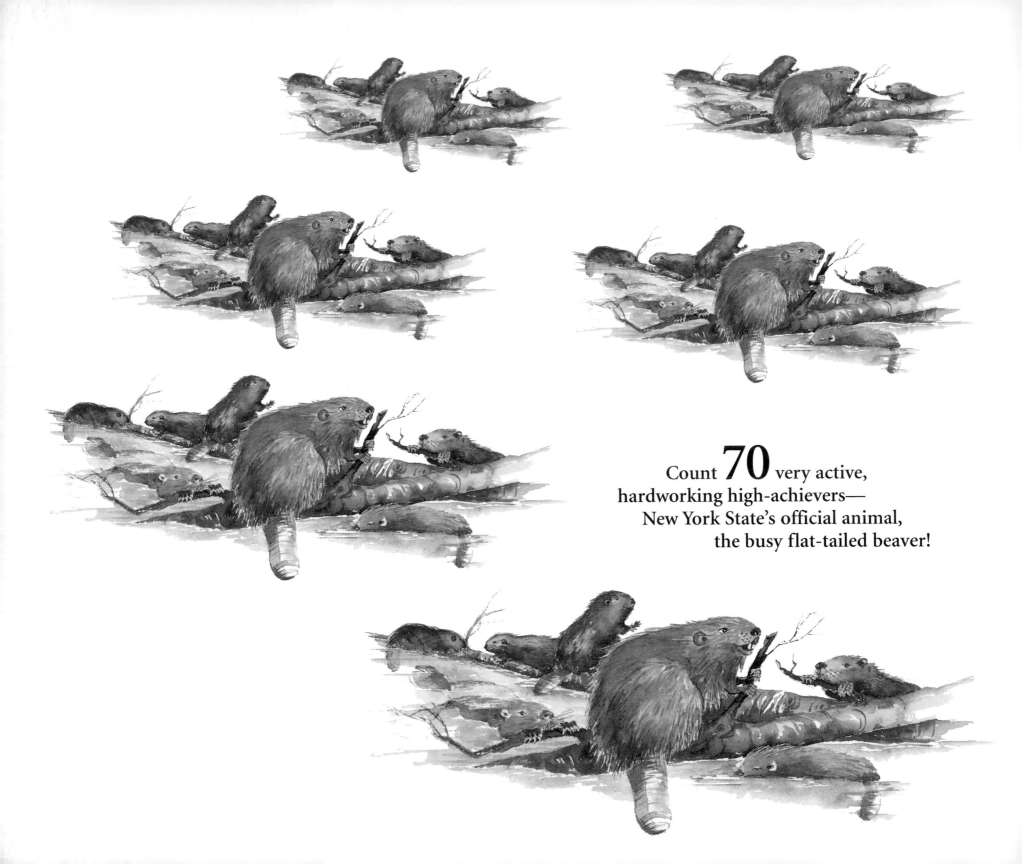

Count **70** very active,
hardworking high-achievers—
New York State's official animal,
the busy flat-tailed beaver!

The beaver is North America's largest rodent. It has a wide, flat, oar-like tail, and two protruding teeth that are strong enough to gnaw down trees. The beaver uses trees, branches, and mud to build dams across rivers and streams. These dams create a deep pool of water in which the beaver builds its home. A beaver home is called a lodge. A baby beaver or "kit" remains in the family lodge until the age of two.

Beaver fur, known as pelt, was once highly popular as a trim for hats and coats. How might the popularity of beaver fur contributed to the colonization of New York?

seventy

70

Mary Edwards Walker was born in Oswego in 1832. An individualist, Mary thought that the long heavy garments that women traditionally wore were cumbersome and unhealthy. Her decision to wear trousers beneath her shortened dress caused her to be ridiculed and even arrested!

Mary graduated from Syracuse Medical College, and during the Civil War tried to enlist as an army surgeon. Woman doctors were not widely accepted, and her repeated requests were denied. Disappointed but undaunted, Mary cared for the sick as a volunteer and was eventually contracted as a *civilian* surgeon.

In 1866 Dr. Mary Edwards Walker received the Congressional Medal of Honor, our country's highest military award. She remains the only woman to have received it. In 1982 the United States Postal Service honored her with a postage stamp recognizing her contributions as a humanitarian, a patriot, and a suffragette.

eighty
80

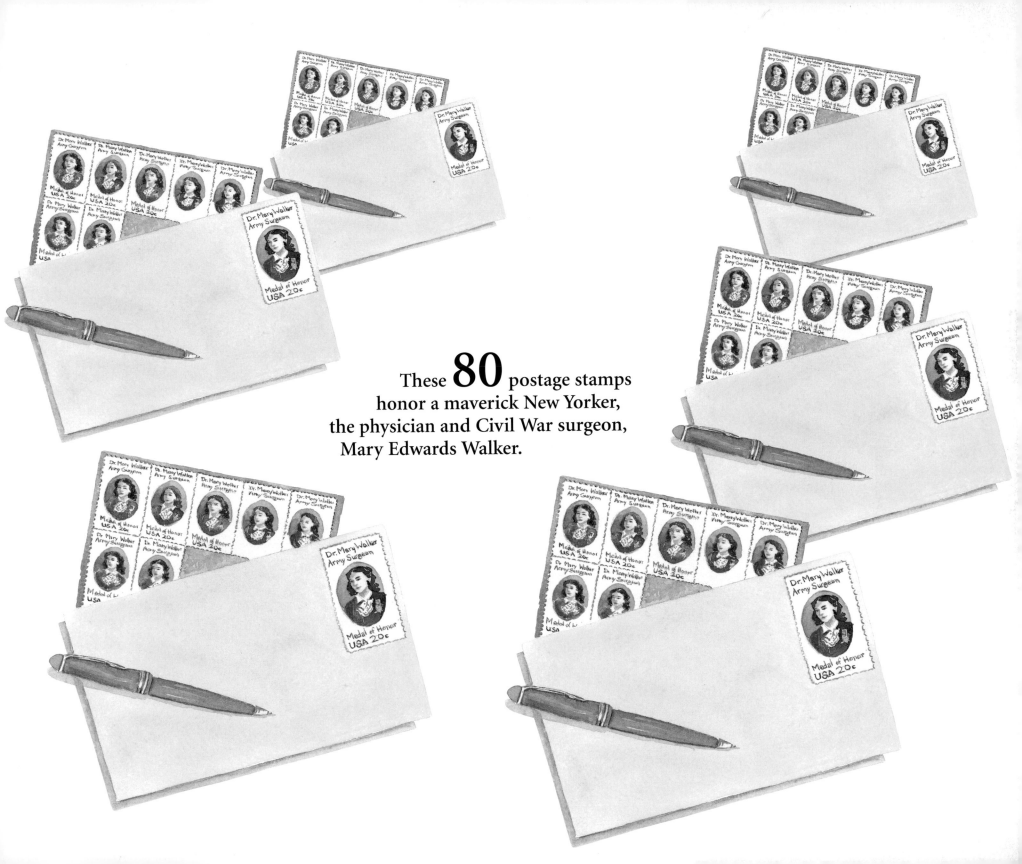

These **80** postage stamps
honor a maverick New Yorker,
the physician and Civil War surgeon,
Mary Edwards Walker.

These **90** pointed leaves
blowing in the breeze
are from New York State's
sap-producing sugar maple tree.

The sugar maple tree is a deciduous tree whose trunk yields an amber-colored sap that is boiled down to make maple syrup. It takes about 40 gallons of sap to make one gallon of syrup.

New York is the third-leading maple producer in the country. In 1977 the American Maple Museum was founded in Lewis County, New York. The American Maple Museum showcases the history and development of North American maple syrup.

Although the sugar maple tree was declared our state tree in 1956, it was important to New York long before the twentieth century. Native Americans made maple syrup before Europeans arrived on this continent, and maple sugar was the most popular sweetener used by the early colonists.

ninety
90

Between March 11 and March 14, 1888, a ferocious snowstorm hit the East Coast. Across New York snowdrifts reached the tops of houses and trees. In rural areas tunnels were dug from farmhouses to barns so that animals would not starve. Because they lived closer to nature, however, people in the country seemed better prepared than city people to deal with this unexpected blizzard. In New York City, telegraph and telephone wires were so weighted down that communication was totally cut off. Trains could not run. People who usually shopped at the market every day were suddenly stranded without food.

The Blizzard of 1888 convinced many people of the importance of an underground transportation system. The disaster brought about other reforms as well. After the storm, utility poles were taken down and electric cables were buried underground. Local government recognized the need for organized snow and garbage removal. The blizzard reminded everyone that new technologies bring new responsibilities.

one hundred 100

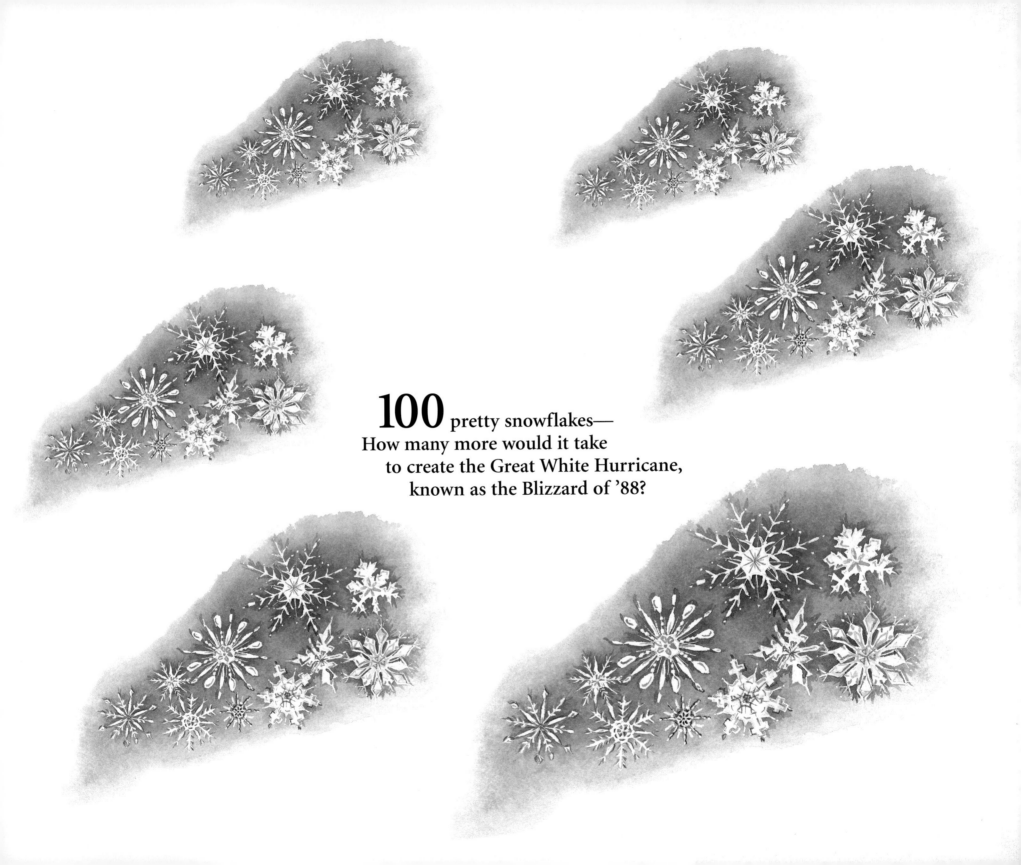

100 pretty snowflakes—
How many more would it take
to create the Great White Hurricane,
known as the Blizzard of '88?

Ann E. Burg

Born in New York, Ann Burg spent her happy early childhood years in Brooklyn where she wrote poetry and read lots of books. She continued to write stories and poems throughout her teaching career and had numerous articles published in newspapers throughout New York and New Jersey.

With the support of her family, Ann decided to pursue her writing full-time. Her first book with Sleeping Bear Press, *E is for Empire: A New York State Alphabet*, was such an adventure that she couldn't wait to begin counting her way back through the state. Ann resides in Albany with her husband Marc, daughter Celia, son Alex, and one very special bear.

Maureen K. Brookfield

Maureen Brookfield is an accomplished artist best known for her watercolor paintings. She loves watercolor's beautiful transparency and finds great joy when painting because of its spontaneity. She lived and studied in the New York/New Jersey area for many years. Maureen attended the Parsons School of Design and the Art Center of Northern New Jersey, and studied with several prominent and nationally known artists. Her work, which has been widely exhibited and won many awards, is in private collections here and abroad, as well as in local galleries. Maureen lives in Marshfield, Massachusetts, and is very active in local and regional art associations. She has also illustrated *E is for Empire: A New York State Alphabet* and *N is for Nutmeg: A Connecticut Alphabet* from Sleeping Bear Press.